I
AM

DRAWINGS BY

MAJANA SA

Copyright © 2024 Majana Sa

All rights reserved.

ISBN: 9798345840764

I AM
I AM

DEDICATION

To God.

I AM

I AM

CONTENTS

Acknowledgments	vii
Introduction	ix
Space	xi
Rest	xiii
Be	xv
Respectful	xvii
Heal	xix
Spectacular	xxi
Enough	xxiii
See	xxv
Without Thought	xxvii
Turn Inwards	xxix
Cut Through Mind	xxxi
Smile	xxxiii
Float Above the Battlefield	xxxv
Unending Presence	xxxvii
Share the Message with Bliss	xxxix
About the Author	xli

I AM
I AM

ACKNOWLEDGMENTS

To my Teacher, Sachi Sa, for encouraging me to title this book 'I AM.'

I AM

I AM

INTRODUCTION

These drawings were created from the heart. Without judgement as to how people will react. Just freehand. Literally, I let my hand be free as it moved with a drawing utensil across the blank page. What will be created? I focused atop of my head, in the crown chakra and allowed the hand to move freely. And when it seemed appropriate, I asked within, while focusing above my head, is this drawing complete? And the head would nod yes or no.

This is how I go about my day. The head nod is a wonderful practice to get to know your Higher Self, the Master Self within Your Own Presence. It is a gentle, kind, formidable Presence that is available to All. It is a Guide, created by God, to help you in your journey from individuality, to unity in God. It is Your Guide to God. You may have sensed Its Presence previously, as it had a sense of All Knowingness, and Unconditional Love. Always guiding us on the right path, for the fastest way Home, to our Eternal Reality of the Almighty Father in Heaven.

I hope this book inspires you to look within and find the Eternal Presence of the Master Self, Your Helper on your journey Home.

With Love,

Majana

I AM
I AM

x
x

I AM
I AM

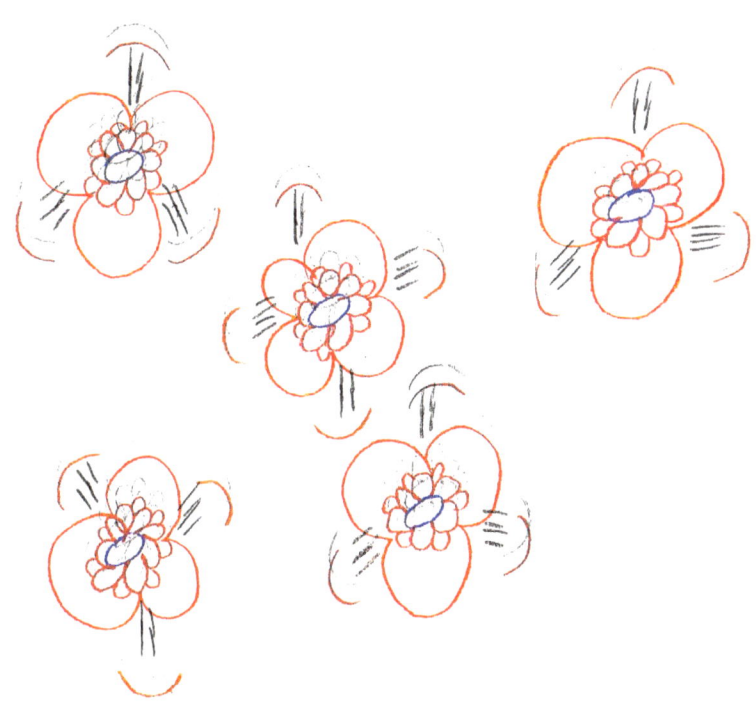

I AM

I AM

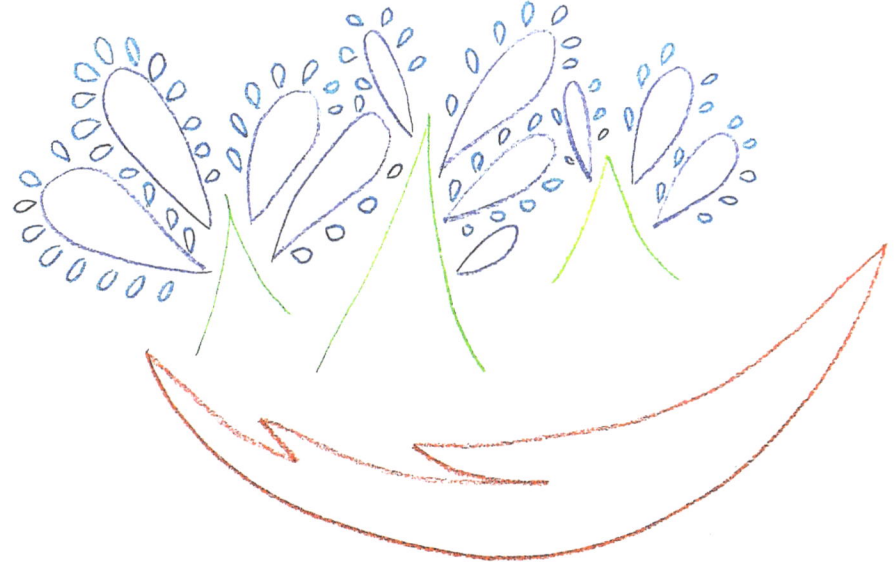

I AM
I AM

I AM
I AM

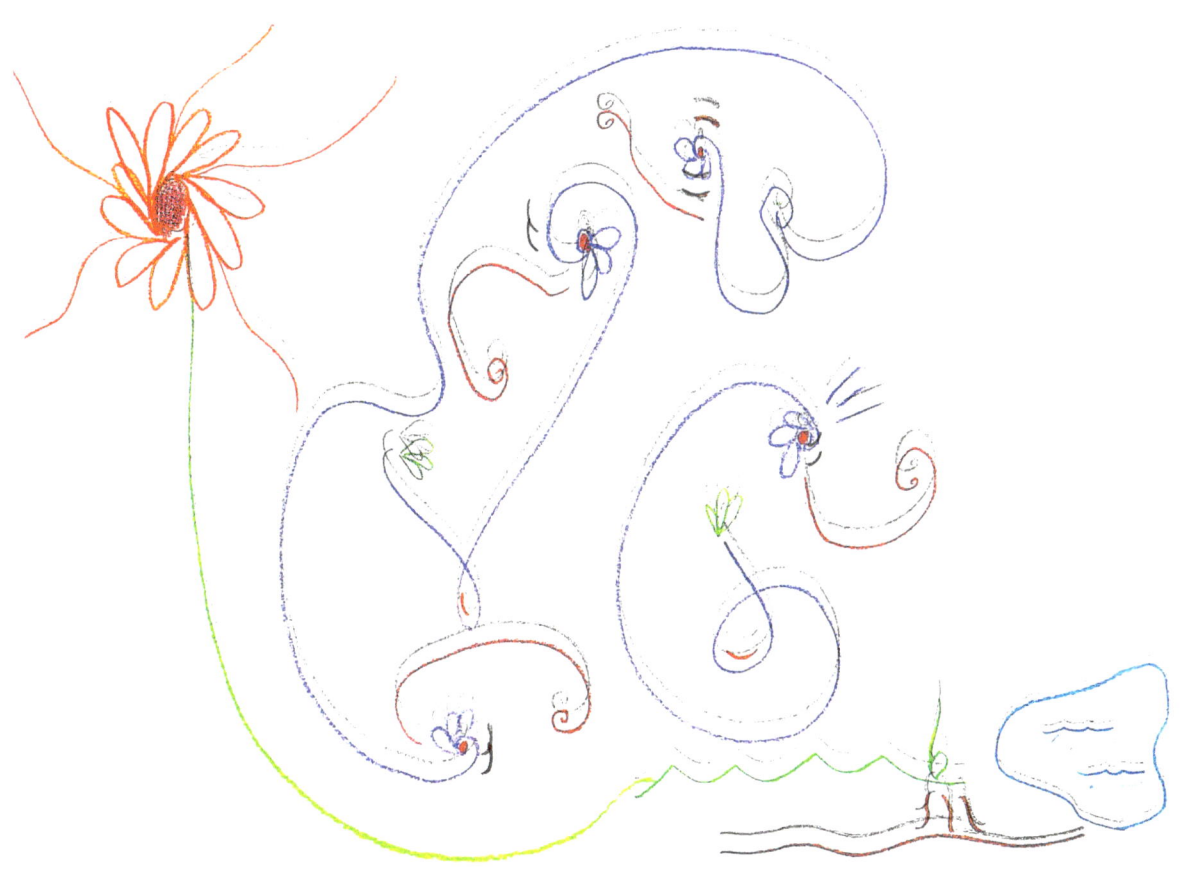

I AM

I AM

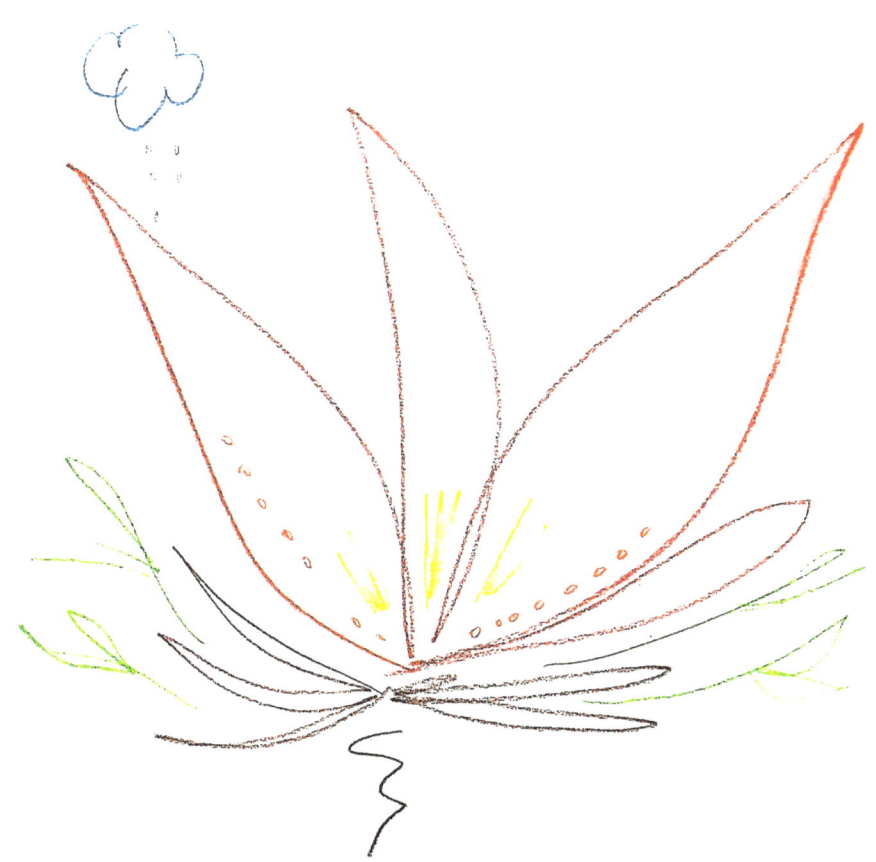

I AM
I AM

I AM
I AM

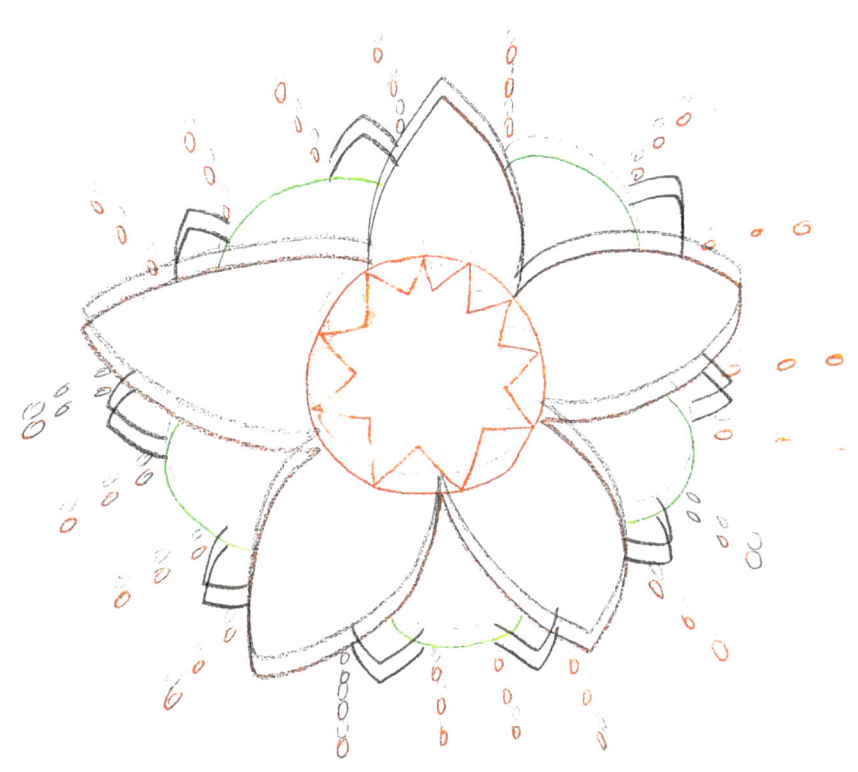

I AM

I AM

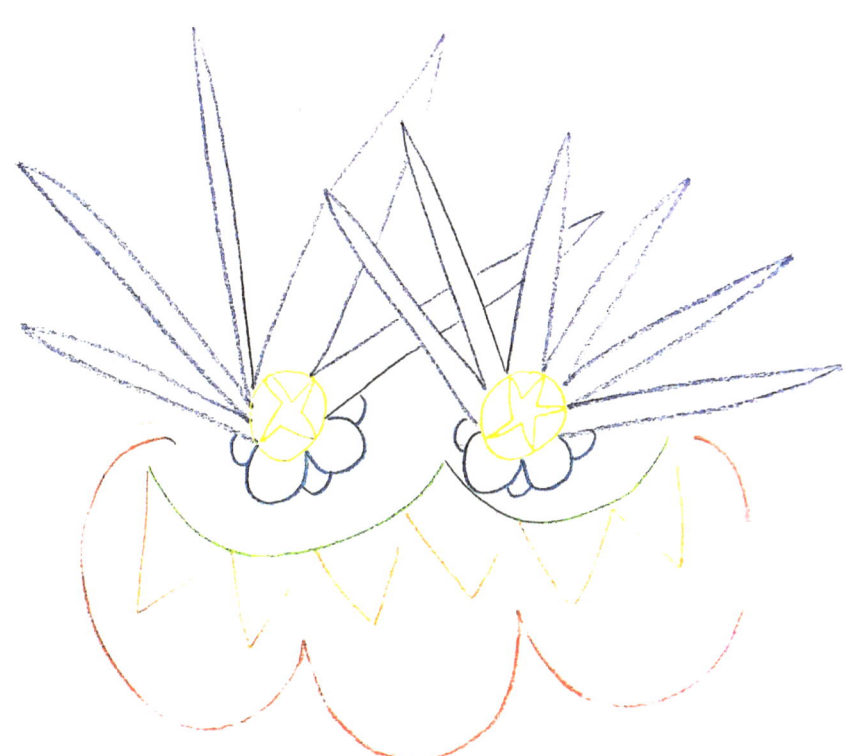

I AM
I AM

I AM
I AM

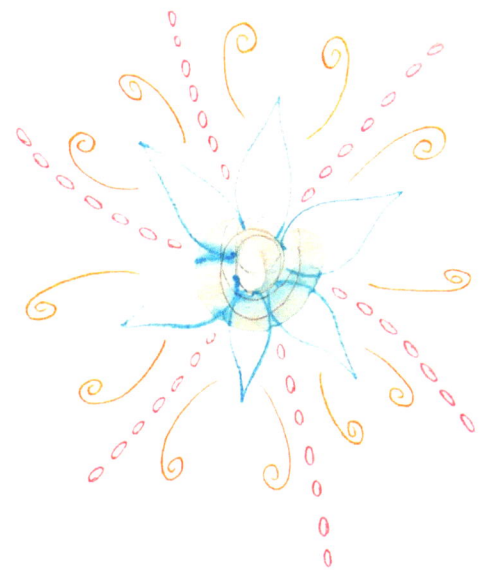

xxiii
xxiii

I AM

I AM

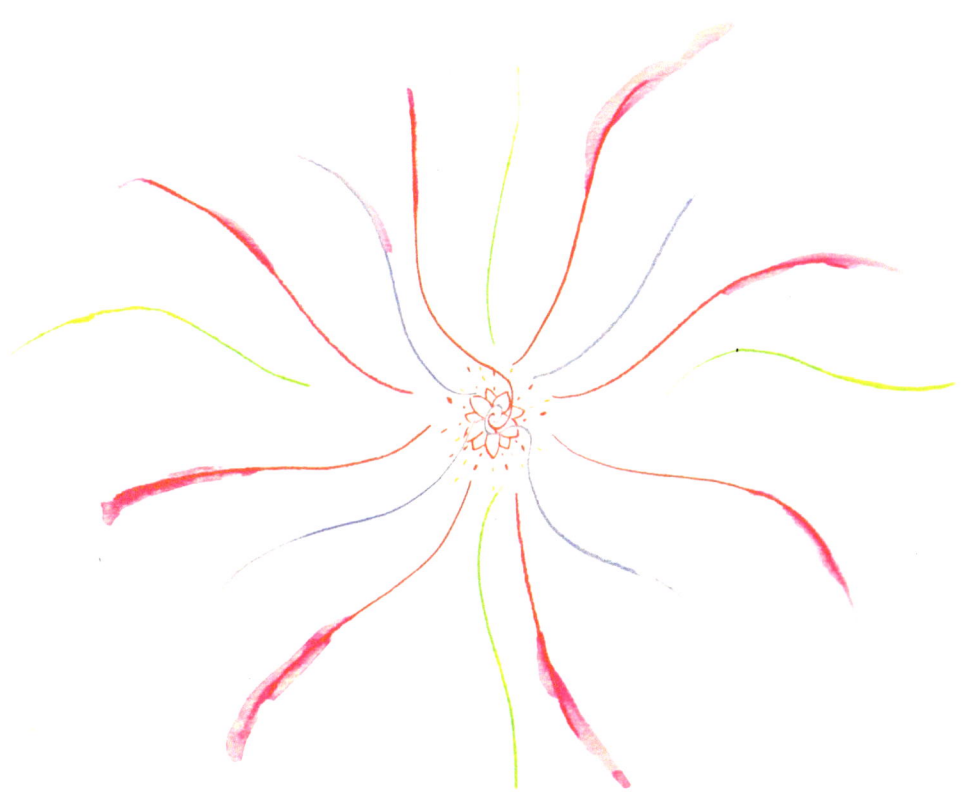

I AM
I AM

I AM
I AM

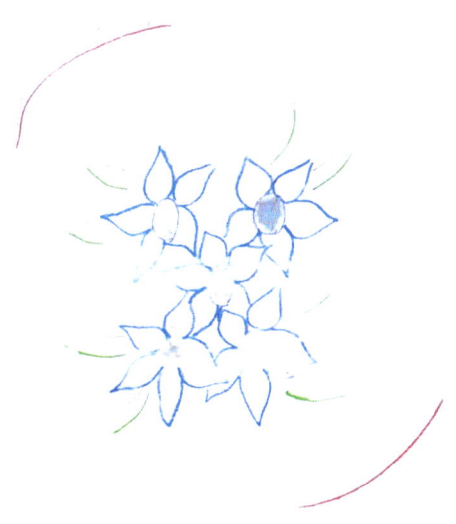

xxvii
xxvii

I AM

I AM

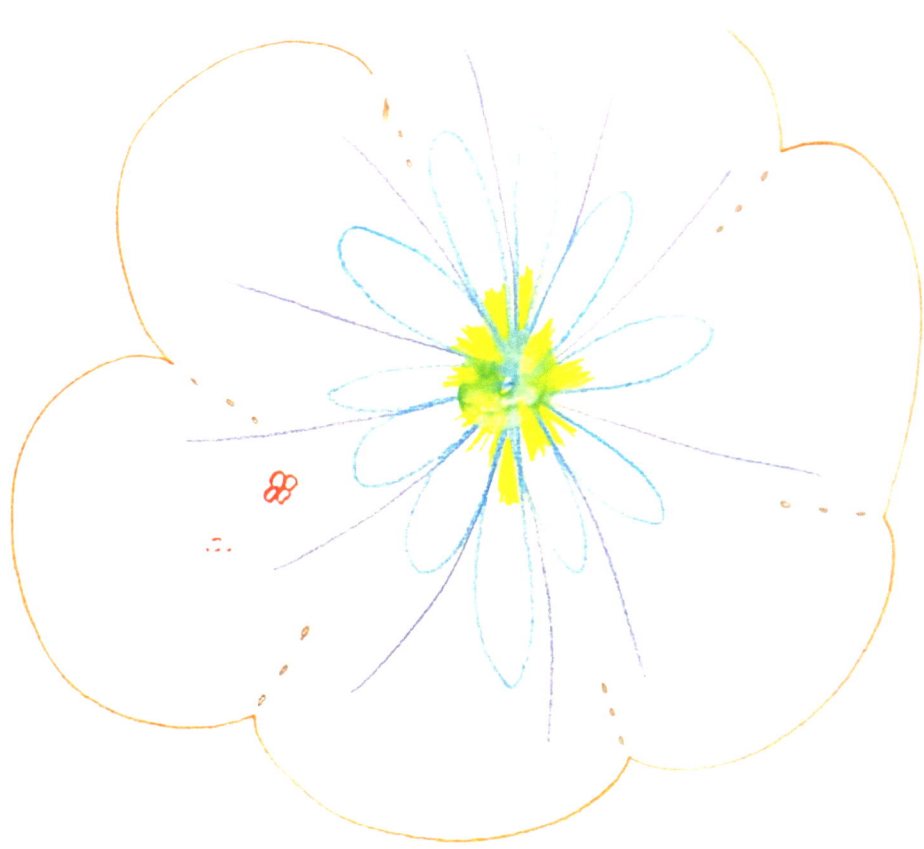

I AM
I AM

xxx
xxx

I AM
I AM

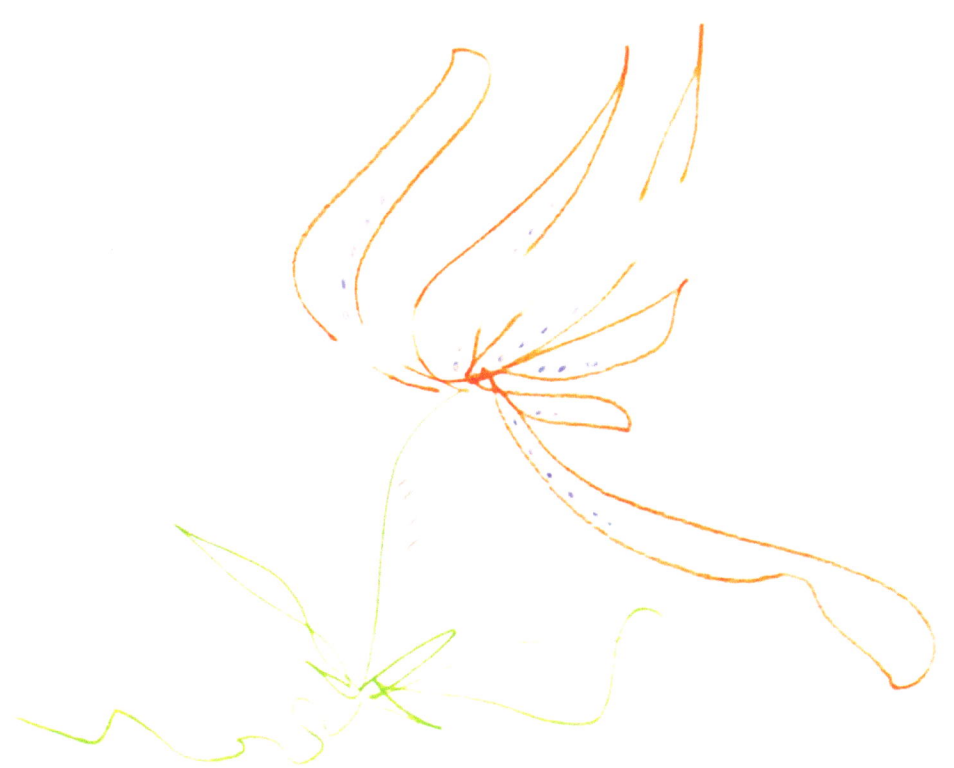

xxxi
xxxi

I AM

I AM

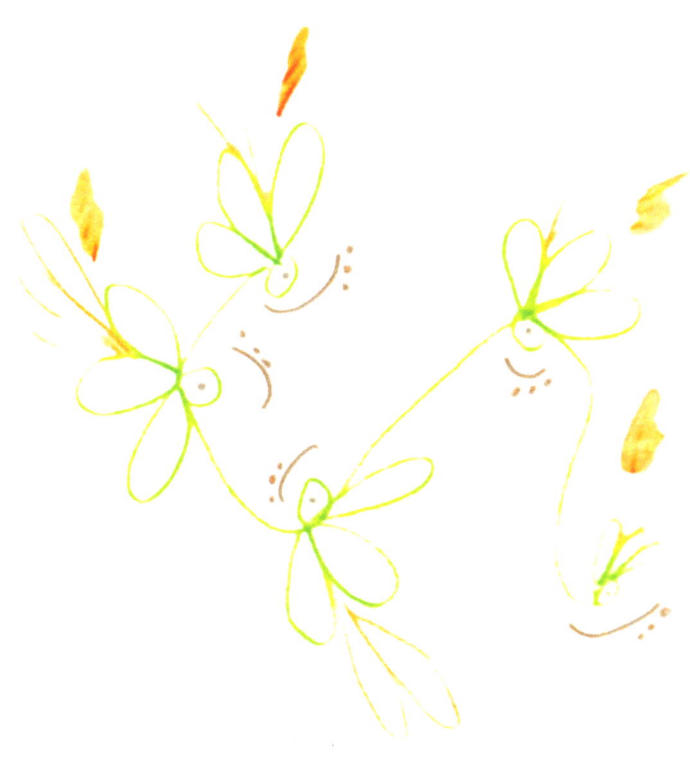

I AM
I AM

I AM
I AM

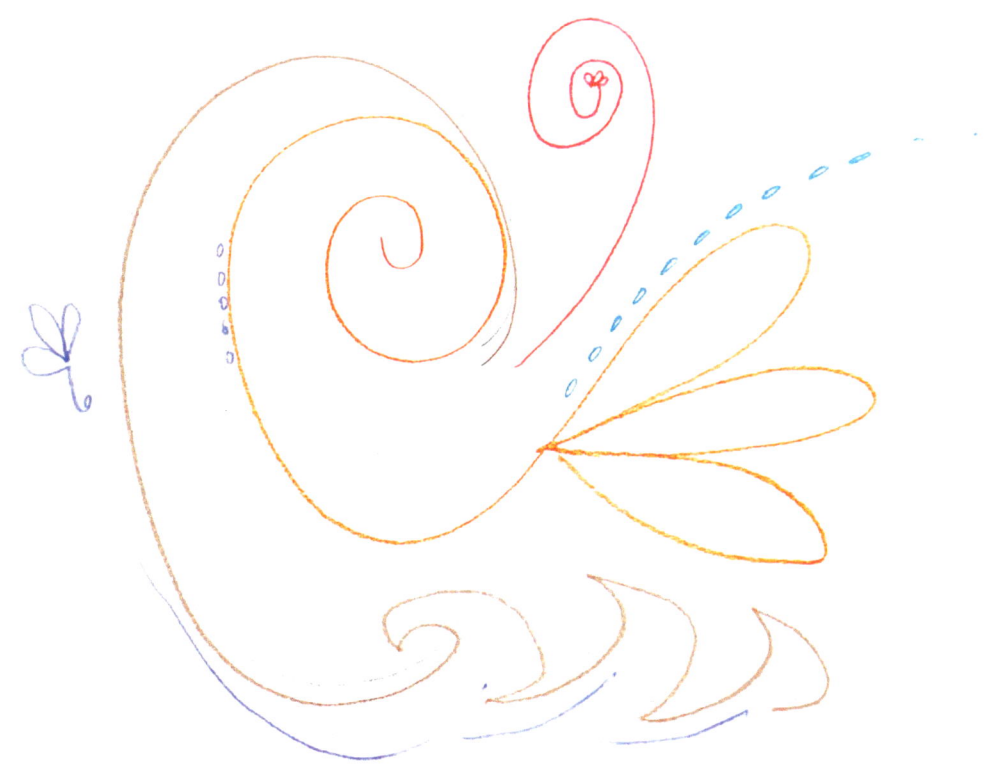

I AM

I AM

I AM
I AM

I AM
I AM

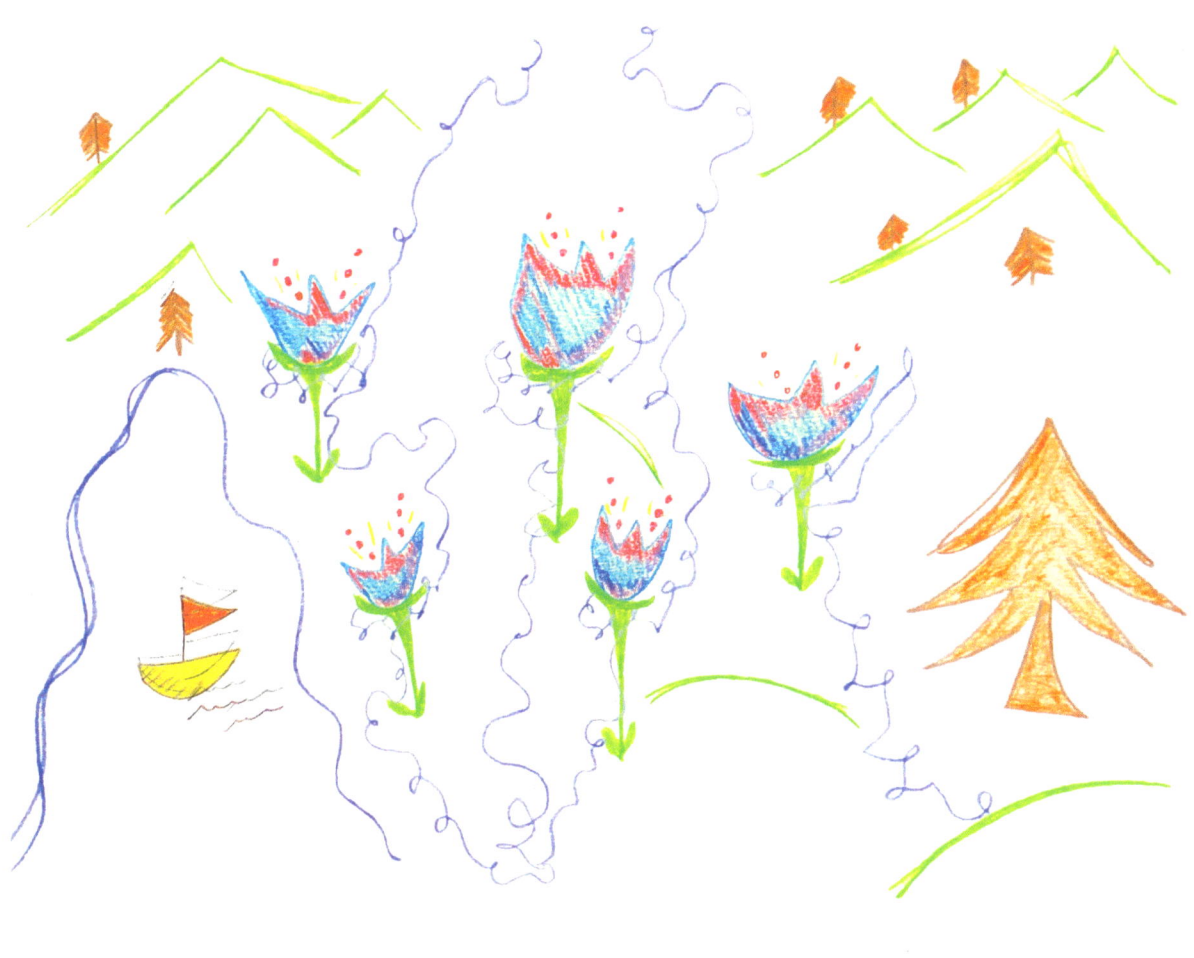

I AM

ABOUT THE AUTHOR

Majana enjoys writing poetry, drawing art pieces, learning languages, world travel, gardening, and communing with Master Self and God within.
She lives in Kotor, Montenegro, with her Husband and Teacher, Sachi.

I AM
I AM

www.ingramcontent.com/pod-product-compliance
Lightning Source LLC
Chambersburg PA
CBHW051931210526
45473CB00006B/2207